The Story of Harriet Tubman

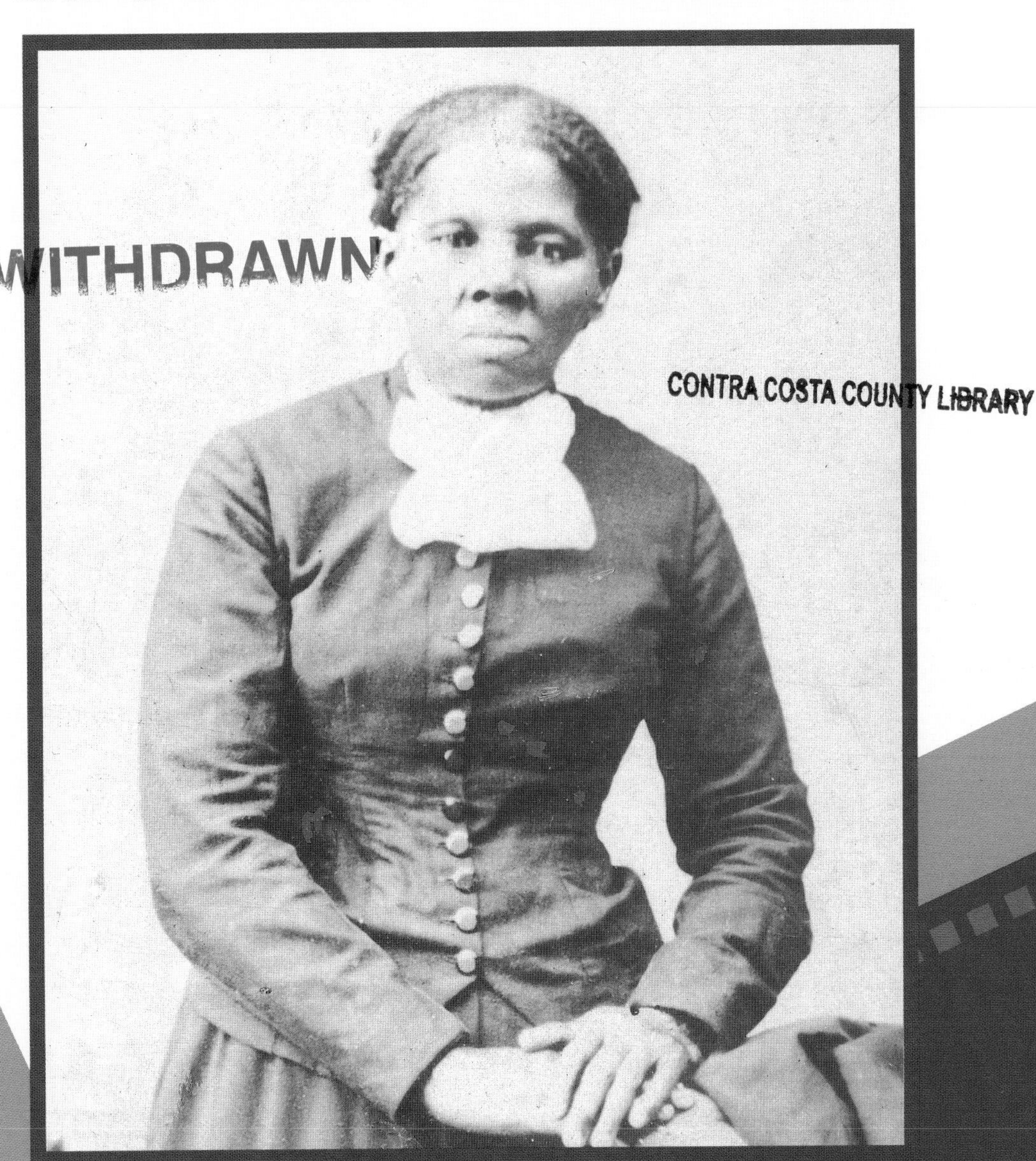

by Rachel A. Koestler-Grack

CHELSEA CLUBHOUSE
An Imprint of Chelsea House Publishers
A Haights Cross Communications Company
Philadelphia

Chelsea Clubhouse books are published by Chelsea House Publishers, a subsidiary of Haights Cross Communications

A Haights Cross Communications Company

The Chelsea House World Wide Web address is www.chelseahouse.com

Printed and bound in the United States of America.
9 8 7 6 5 4 3 2 1

Library of Congress Cataloging-in-Publication Data
Koestler-Grack, Rachel A., 1973–
The story of Harriet Tubman / by Rachel A. Koestler-Grack.
p. cm. — (Breakthrough biographies)
Summary: A biography of American abolitionist Harriet Tubman, who escaped slavery and led others to freedom as a conductor on the Underground Railroad. Includes bibliographical references and index.
ISBN 0-7910-7314-9
1. Tubman, Harriet, 1820?–1913—Juvenile literature. 2. Slaves—United States—Biography—Juvenile literature.
3. African American women—Biography—Juvenile literature. 4. Underground railroad—Juvenile literature. [1. Tubman, Harriet, 1820?–1913. 2. Slaves. 3. African Americans—Biography. 4. Women—Biography. 5. Underground railroad.
6. Antislavery movements.] I. Title. II. Series.
E444.T82.K64 2004
973.918'092–dc21 2003000271

Selected Sources

This book reflects newly discovered information about Harriet Tubman as researched and documented by Kate Clifford Larson in the biography *Bound for the Promised Land: Harriet Tubman, Portrait of an American Hero*. New York: Ballantine Books, 2003.

Other sources include:

Bentley, Judith. *Harriet Tubman*. New York: Franklin Watts, 1990.

Blockson, Charles L. *The Underground Railroad*. New York: Prentice-Hall, 1987.

Bradford, Sarah. *Harriet Tubman: The Moses of Her People*. Gloucester, Mass.: Peter Smith/Corinth, 1981.

Conrad, Earl. *Harriet Tubman*. New York: Paul S. Eriksson, Inc., 1969.

Editorial Credits

Colleen Sexton, editor; Takeshi Takahashi, designer; Mary Englar, photo researcher; Jennifer Krassy Peiler, layout

Content Reviewer

Kate Clifford Larson, Ph.D., author of *Bound for the Promised Land: Harriet Tubman, Portrait of an American Hero*. New York: Ballantine Books, 2003.

Photo Credits

Hulton/Archive by Getty Images: cover, 6, 7, 13 (bottom), 14, 17, 18, 19 (bottom), 20 (bottom), 29 (Amelia Bloomer and Sojourner Truth); Library of Congress: title page, 10, 20 (top); Smithsonian American Art Museum/Art Resource: 4, 12; ©CORBIS: 5, 13 (top), 22, 23; E.O. Hoppe/©CORBIS: 8 (top); Richard Cummins/©CORBIS: 8 (bottom); Stock Montage, Inc.: 9; Schomburg Center for Research in Black Culture, New York Public Library/Astor, Lenox and Tilden Foundations: 21, 24; "Harriet Tubman's Underground Railroad," by world-renowned artist Paul Collins—www.collinsart.com: 15; Bettmann/©CORBIS: 16, 29 (Emily Dickinson); National Archives: 19 (top), 26; Cayuga County Historian: 25; AP/Wide World: 29 (Elizabeth Blackwell); National Library of Medicine: 29 (Clara Barton); Rick Apitz: back cover.

Table of Contents

A Dangerous Trip

On Christmas Eve, 1854, Harriet Tubman hid in an old shed used to store feed for animals. The shed was just outside her parents' home on the Eastern Shore of Maryland, a slave state. Harriet was a runaway slave. She had secretly traveled back to her family from her new home in Pennsylvania, a free state. Three of her brothers were to be sold at a slave **auction** in two days. Harriet planned to take them north to freedom instead.

At that time, slavery was legal in most Southern states. White people could own black people as their property. Owners could force blacks to work or sell them for money. Many slaves, including Harriet's family, worked on large farms called plantations. They lived in small cabins in the slave quarters but spent long hours laboring in the fields or serving their owner's family in the "big house."

Artist William H. Johnson painted this portrait of Harriet Tubman as a fighter for freedom. The painting is in the collection of the Smithsonian American Art Museum in Washington, D.C.

Many slaves—including Harriet and her brothers—made their escape at night when they were least likely to be seen.

Harriet had fled from her owner in 1849 and escaped to the Northern states, where slavery was against the law. Traveling back to Maryland was dangerous for Harriet. If she were caught, she could face severe punishment or death. Harriet knew the risks, but she wanted to help her brothers.

Harriet and her brothers left the next night for Pennsylvania. They knew the plantation owner would send slave catchers after them. These men traveled with guns and dogs, hunting down runaway slaves. Harriet and her brothers had to stay out of sight. The group traveled at night under cover of darkness. Along the way, they stopped at safe houses. People who lived in these homes believed slavery was wrong. They provided food for Harriet and her brothers and hid them in secret rooms during the day. After several nights of dangerous travel through Maryland and Delaware, Harriet and her brothers crossed into Pennsylvania. They were free. Harriet would make this daring trip to the South again and again to help other slaves escape.

Growing Up a Slave

Harriet Tubman was born a slave in Dorchester County, Maryland. No one is sure of her exact date of birth, but historians believe it was sometime in early 1822. She was one of nine children born to Benjamin Ross and Harriet Green, who were known as "Ben" and "Rit." Rit named her daughter Araminta Ross and called her "Minty." Young Minty was owned by Edward Brodess. She lived with her family in the slave quarters on his plantation.

When Minty was about 5 years old, Brodess started hiring her out. She worked for other people, and the money she earned went to her owner. At one plantation, she spent her days wading in shallow river waters, checking animal traps. The water was icy cold, and Minty had only thin clothes to wear. She soon became sick with a fever and was sent back to her mother.

This slave family in South Carolina probably lived and worked on a plantation, just as Harriet's family did. Other slaves were craftspeople, such as cabinetmakers and blacksmiths. Slaves also labored in factories, built railroads, and worked in mines.

> *"I grew up like a weed—ignorant of liberty, having no experience of it. I was not happy or contented. Every time I saw a white man, I was afraid of being carried away. We were always uneasy."*
>
> —Harriet Tubman

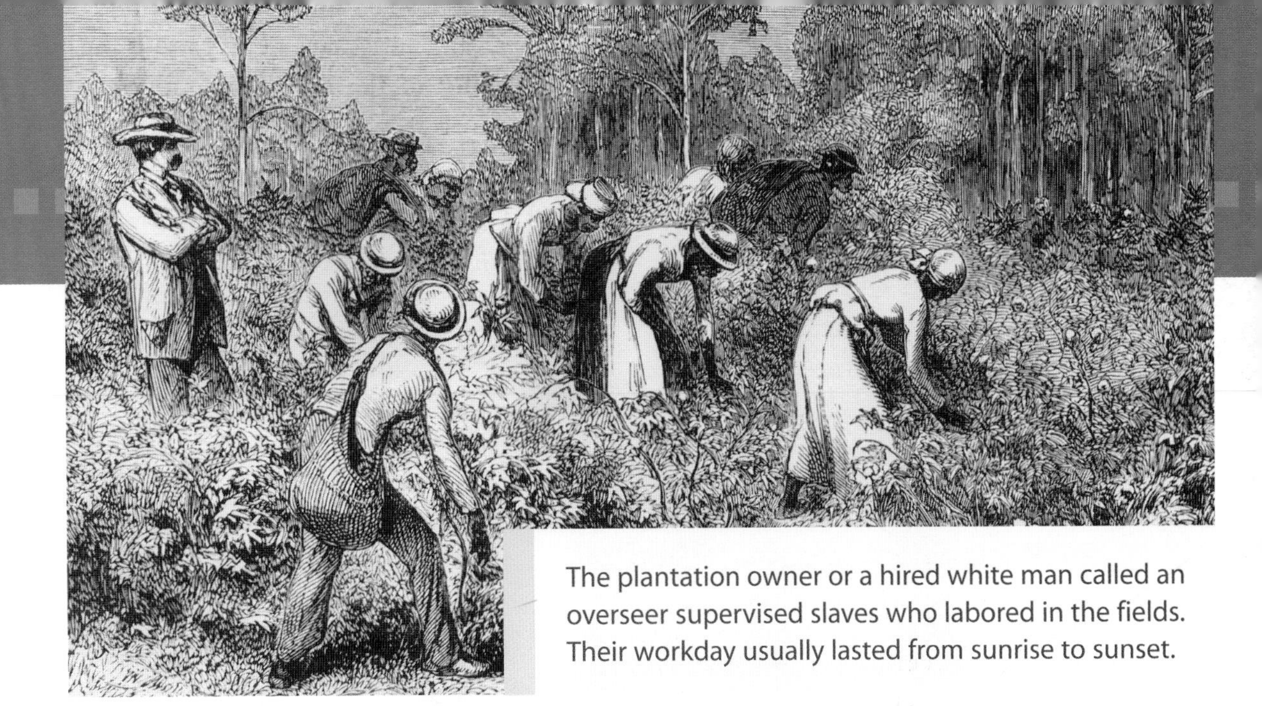

The plantation owner or a hired white man called an overseer supervised slaves who labored in the fields. Their workday usually lasted from sunrise to sunset.

Minty went to work at another plantation when she was 7 years old. She received only table scraps to eat and was always hungry. One morning she tried to take a sugar cube, but she was caught. Frightened, Minty ran from the house until she was too tired to run anymore. She stayed in a pigpen for four days, fighting with the young pigs for potato peelings and other scraps. Hungry and tired, Minty finally decided to return to the house. She received a whipping and was sent back to the Brodess plantation.

Minty grew into a strong, hardworking young woman. She was also strong-willed. One evening in about 1835, when Minty was around 13 years old, she was working in the cornfields with a group of slaves. A slave boy snuck away from the group. A white **overseer** went after him, carrying a whip. Minty followed them. The overseer caught up with the boy at a store and then noticed Minty. He told her to help tie up the boy, but Minty refused. The boy took off running again. Outraged, the overseer picked up a lead weight and threw it at the boy. But the weight hit Minty in the head instead. She fell to the ground **unconscious**.

A plantation's slave quarters was made up of small, roughly built cabins (left). Inside a cabin (below), slaves usually slept on a hard floor with only thin blankets for warmth. Some cabins had fireplaces, where meals could be cooked.

Rit nursed Minty for weeks. But her daughter would not wake up. While Minty slept, she had the same dream over and over. She was flying above fields and rivers. Beautiful women dressed in white stretched out their arms to her. They showed Minty a line that separated slavery and freedom. In the land of freedom, miles of green fields and flowers lay before her. Minty heard the words, "Come. Arise. Flee for your life."

Finally, Minty woke up. Many months passed before she was able to walk without help. She had a scar and a dent in her forehead. For the rest of her life, she had headaches and would suddenly fall into a deep sleep in the middle of whatever she was doing.

Slavery in the South

In the late 1600s, slave traders began bringing Africans to the American colonies. Slave traders kidnapped men, women, and children in West Africa. They put the Africans in chains and forced them aboard ships bound for America. When the boats reached America, slave traders sold those who survived the journey to white owners throughout the colonies.

By the late 1700s, most slaves were working on plantations in the South. Slaves labored long hours six days a week. Plantation owners often whipped slaves who complained. Families lived in crude, one-room cabins in a separate area of the plantation called the slave quarters. The cabins were cold in the winter and hot in the summer. Most slaves didn't have enough to eat. Plantation owners usually supplied only small amounts of milk, cornmeal, and pork.

At age 5 or 6, slave children began working on the plantation. By the time they were 10 years old, the children worked a full day, just like the adult slaves. Owners often sold slave children, forcing them to leave their parents at a young age. Many children never saw their parents again.

At auctions, buyers looked for young, strong slaves who could work hard. They often examined a slave like they would an animal, making sure the "property" was healthy. Slaves were then sold to the buyer who bid the most money.

Follow the North Star

Minty was changed by her injury and by her dreams. She now knew in her heart that she was meant to be free. Minty began praying, asking God to change people's beliefs about slavery. She prayed especially hard for her owner. Over and over, she said, "Oh Lord, convert ole master; change that man's heart!"

By the spring of 1836, Minty was able to work again. She was hired out as a field worker at a nearby plantation. She met slaves from the surrounding community. From them, she heard stories about the Underground Railroad. This secret system of people and safe houses helped slaves reach freedom in the North. The stories excited Minty, but they also made her uneasy. She knew escaping would be difficult.

Like many slaves, Harriet believed strongly in prayer. She said she always felt God was with her, leading her and protecting her.

A runaway slave's "ticket" for the Underground Railroad was usually a note from one helper, or "agent," to another. This photograph shows the original handwritten ticket at the top and a typed version at the bottom.

A TICKET ON THE UNDERGROUND RAILROAD

"Medina Sept 6 1858
Prof. Monroe and Peck
Gents, here are five Slaves from the House of Bondage, which I need not say to you that you will see to them—they can tell their own story

Yours etc
H. G. Blake"

In 1844, at age 22, Minty married John Tubman. It was at this time that she took the name Harriet and became known as Harriet Tubman. Her new husband was a free black. His parents had been freed by their owner, so he was free, too. Even though she married a free man, Harriet was still a slave. She went home to her husband's cabin only after she had finished the day's work for her owner. Harriet often talked about freedom, but her husband tried to discourage her. He was already free, and he wasn't interested in going north.

In 1849, Harriet's owner died, and she learned she would soon be sold. The time had come to run away. "No one will take me back alive," she told herself. Harriet crept out of the cabin at night while her husband slept. Outside, she looked up at the sky and saw the North Star shining brightly. The star would lead her to freedom.

"There was one of two things I had a right to, liberty or death; if I could not have one, I would have the other; for no man should take me alive."

—Harriet Tubman

First, Harriet went to see a white woman who lived nearby. Harriet knew the woman would help her escape. The woman told Harriet where to go next and gave her a piece of paper with words written on it. It was Harriet's first "ticket" for the Underground Railroad.

Artist James Michael Newell painted this scene of the Underground Railroad. As dawn approaches, farmers help hide a family of escaped slaves in a cave.

Near dawn, Harriet reached the next "station." She softly knocked on the door and a woman answered. Harriet gave the note to the woman, who then handed Harriet a broom and told her to sweep the walk. Harriet was confused. She wondered if she had been tricked into being this woman's slave. But Harriet soon learned that the work would protect her. Slave catchers would not suspect she was a runaway if she were working. The woman's husband was a farmer. That night, he took Harriet to the next stop. She lay in the back of his wagon covered with vegetables. Harriet was impressed by the clever methods people used to hide her.

During Harriet's journey North, other "agents" on the Underground Railroad helped her. Following the North Star, she traveled through many miles of woods and swamps. After traveling for about a week, she arrived in Pennsylvania. Harriet was finally standing on free soil. She later remembered, "I looked at my hands to see if I was the same person now that I was free. There was such a glory over everything; the sun came like gold through the trees, and over the fields, and I felt like I was in heaven."

The Abolition Movement

At rallies in the North, abolitionists drew crowds with their fiery speeches opposing slavery.

Abolitionists believed slavery was wrong and worked to end it. The movement to end slavery began in colonial times. A religious group called the **Quakers** said slavery was immoral. They worked to change people's beliefs about slavery. Some politicians began to speak out against slavery, too. After America won its independence in 1783, many people felt strongly about freedom for all people. States in the North began passing laws to end slavery. By the mid-1800s, the slave states were all in the South.

In 1831, abolitionist William Lloyd Garrison began publishing a newspaper called *The Liberator* in Boston, Massachusetts. He called for an immediate end to slavery. Two years later, the American Anti-Slavery Society was formed to support Garrison's mission. The abolition movement spread. Some leaders entered politics and founded the Liberty Party in 1840 to fight slavery. Others led protests or became part of the Underground Railroad.

By the start of the Civil War in 1861, about 4 million slaves lived in the South. Abolitionists rallied behind the Union during the war. They did whatever they could to help the cause. In 1865, the end of the Civil War freed the slaves. Abolitionists celebrated when the 13th Amendment to the Constitution was passed that year. It outlawed slavery throughout the country.

In his newspaper, *The Liberator*, abolitionist William Lloyd Garrison called for an end to slavery.

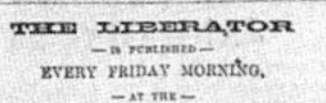

THE LIBERATOR
— IS PUBLISHED —
EVERY FRIDAY MORNING,
— AT THE —
ANTI-SLAVERY OFFICE, 21 CORNHILL.

ROBERT F. WALLCUT, General Agent.

☞ TERMS — Two dollars and fifty cents per annum, in advance.
☞ Five copies will be sent to one address for TEN DOLLARS, if payment be made in advance.
☞ All remittances are to be made, and all letters relating to the pecuniary concerns of the paper are to be directed, (POST PAID,) to the General Agent.
☞ Advertisements making less than one square inserted three times for 75 cents — one square for $1.00.
☞ The Agents of the American, Massachusetts, Pennsylvania, Ohio and Michigan Anti-Slavery Societies are authorised to receive subscriptions for THE LIBERATOR.
☞ The following gentlemen constitute the Financial Committee, but are not responsible for any of the debts of the paper, viz:—FRANCIS JACKSON, EDMUND QUINCY, SAMUEL PHILBRICK, and WENDELL PHILLIPS.

THE LIBERATOR.

NO UNION WITH SLAVEHOLDERS.

The United States Constitution is 'a covenant with death, and an agreement with hell.'

☞ 'The free States are the guardians and essential supports of slavery. We are the jailers and constables of the institution. . . . There is some excuse for communities, when, under a generous impulse, they espouse the cause of the oppressed in other States, and by force restore their rights; but *they are without excuse in aiding other States in binding on men an unrighteous yoke.* On this subject, OUR FATHERS, IN FRAMING THE CONSTITUTION, SWERVED FROM THE RIGHT. We their children, at the end of half a century, see the path of duty more clearly than they, and *must walk in it.* To this point the public mind has long been tending, and the time has come for looking at it fully, dispassionately, and with manly and Christian resolution. . . . No blessing of the Union can be a compensation for taking part in the enslaving of our fellow-creatures; nor ought this bond to be perpetuated, if experience shall demonstrate that it can only continue through our participation in wrong doing. To this conviction the free States are tending.'
— WILLIAM ELLERY CHANNING.

WM. LLOYD GARRISON, Editor. | Our Country is the World, our Countrymen are all Mankind. | J. B. YERRINTON & SON, Printers.

VOL. XXIX. NO. 3. | BOSTON, FRIDAY, JANUARY 21, 1859. | WHOLE NUMBER, 1576.

The Moses of Her People

Harriet was free, but she knew she wouldn't be truly happy until her family was free, too. She decided to make a home for them and then return to the South to help them escape. First she had to find a job. Openings for cooks, dishwashers, and housekeepers were plentiful. Harriet held many of these positions, enjoying the fact that she could quit one job and choose another.

A year after she arrived in Pennsylvania, Harriet learned that her niece Kessiah was to be sold at a slave auction. Kessiah and her husband, John Bowley, had two children. A trip south was dangerous for Harriet, but she had to help the family escape. She made a plan to meet them in Baltimore, Maryland. When the family arrived at a safe house there, they knocked on the door. Someone on the other side asked, "Who is it?" John responded with the Underground Railroad code, "A friend with friends." The door opened and there was Harriet, ready to lead them north to freedom.

After arriving in Pennsylvania, Harriet made her way to Philadelphia. By the early 1850s, this city had the largest black community in the country. Here, an escaped slave could find safety and help in looking for a job.

As a conductor on the Underground Railroad, Harriet often led escaped slaves through swamps. Slave hunters' dogs couldn't pick up the scent of the slaves in the water.

From that time on, Harriet committed herself to helping slaves escape. She soon became a **"conductor"** on the Underground Railroad. Between 1850 and 1860, she made between 11 and 13 trips back to Maryland and freed about 70 slaves. Most were friends and family members, including her parents and four brothers. Harriet later told people, "I can say what most conductors can't say—I never ran my train off the track and I never lost a passenger."

> *"I had crossed the line of which I had so long been dreaming. I was free, but there was no one to welcome me to the land of freedom. I was a stranger in a strange land."*
>
> —Harriet Tubman

No other escaped slaves dared return to a slave state to rescue others. Only Harriet had this courage. She became known as the "**Moses** of her people." Like the Biblical Moses who led the Israelites out of slavery in Egypt, Harriet led black slaves from the South to the North.

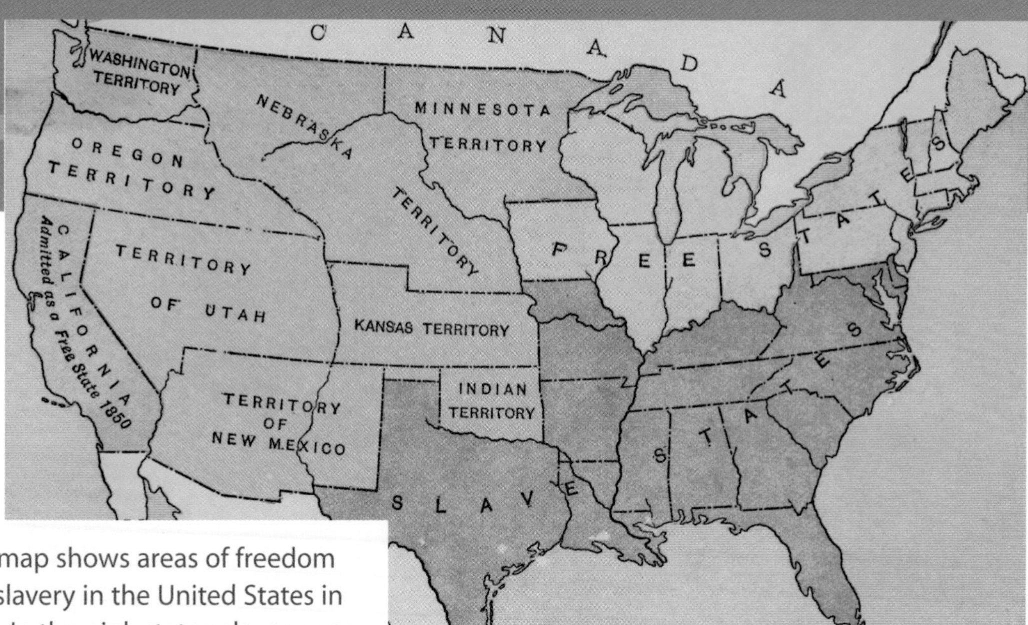

This map shows areas of freedom and slavery in the United States in 1854. In the pink states, slavery was against the law. Slavery was legal in the states shown in dark green. By law, the settlers who lived in the light green areas could choose slavery or freedom for blacks when their territory became a state.

Harriet found clever ways to help runaway slaves. She always led them away from plantations on Saturdays. Runaway notices were not printed in newspapers until the following Monday. There was more time for travel before slave catchers began their search. Harriet often sang to communicate messages and to calm the fears of the escaped slaves. Sometimes runaways wanted to turn back. But Harriet wouldn't let that happen. She would pull out her gun, point it at the runaway, and offer a choice. "Live North or die here," she would say.

By 1860, tension was growing between the North and the South over the issue of slavery. Abraham Lincoln was elected president. He sided with the North against slavery. Many Southerners worried that he would outlaw slavery completely. They believed the states should make their own laws about slavery and other issues, not the **federal** government. The anger grew stronger and riots broke out all over the country. Harriet was now well known in both the North and the South. Her friends feared for her life. They took Harriet to safety in Canada against her will.

The Fugitive Slave Law

In 1850, Congress passed the Fugitive Slave Law, which brought great fear to blacks living in the North. Any black person—whether an escaped slave or a free black—could be arrested if a white person said he or she was a runaway. The black person then went before a hearing where an official decided whether the accused was the missing property of a slave owner. There were no judges or juries present at the hearing. The official was paid $5 for every black person he set free and $10 for every black person he returned to a slave owner.

The Fugitive Slave Law caused panic among blacks living in the North. Many headed to Canada, the only place they would be truly safe from capture. Harriet had made only a few trips south before the law was passed. "After that I wouldn't trust Uncle Sam with my people no longer, but I brought them all clear off to Canada," she said. The length of her trips doubled and so did the danger.

CAUTION!!

COLORED PEOPLE

OF BOSTON, ONE & ALL,

You are hereby respectfully CAUTIONED and advised, to avoid conversing with the

Watchmen and Police Officers of Boston,

For since the recent ORDER OF THE MAYOR & ALDERMEN, they are empowered to act as

KIDNAPPERS

AND

Slave Catchers,

And they have already been actually employed in KIDNAPPING, CATCHING, AND KEEPING SLAVES. Therefore, if you value your LIBERTY, and the *Welfare of the Fugitives* among you, *Shun* them in every possible manner, as so many *HOUNDS* on the track of the most unfortunate of your race.

Keep a Sharp Look Out for KIDNAPPERS, and have TOP EYE open.

APRIL 24, 1851.

This handbill, printed in April 1851, warned black citizens in Boston of the Fugitive Slave Law.

A Union Spy

By February 1861, 11 Southern states had left the Union to form their own government. They called their country the Confederate States of America. On April 12, Confederate troops fired on Union troops at Fort Sumter in South Carolina, and the Civil War (1861–1865) began.

Harriet hurried back from Canada, determined to be part of the action. She convinced government officials to send her south to help the Union Army. In early 1862, she arrived in South Carolina. Many slaves had fled their owners when the war started and were now in Union camps. Harriet went to work in a hospital to nurse the escaped slaves. She also helped them find jobs.

On April 12, 1861, Confederate soldiers fired the first shots of the Civil War. They attacked Union troops at Fort Sumter in Charleston, South Carolina. The Confederates took the fort and held it until the end of the war in 1865.

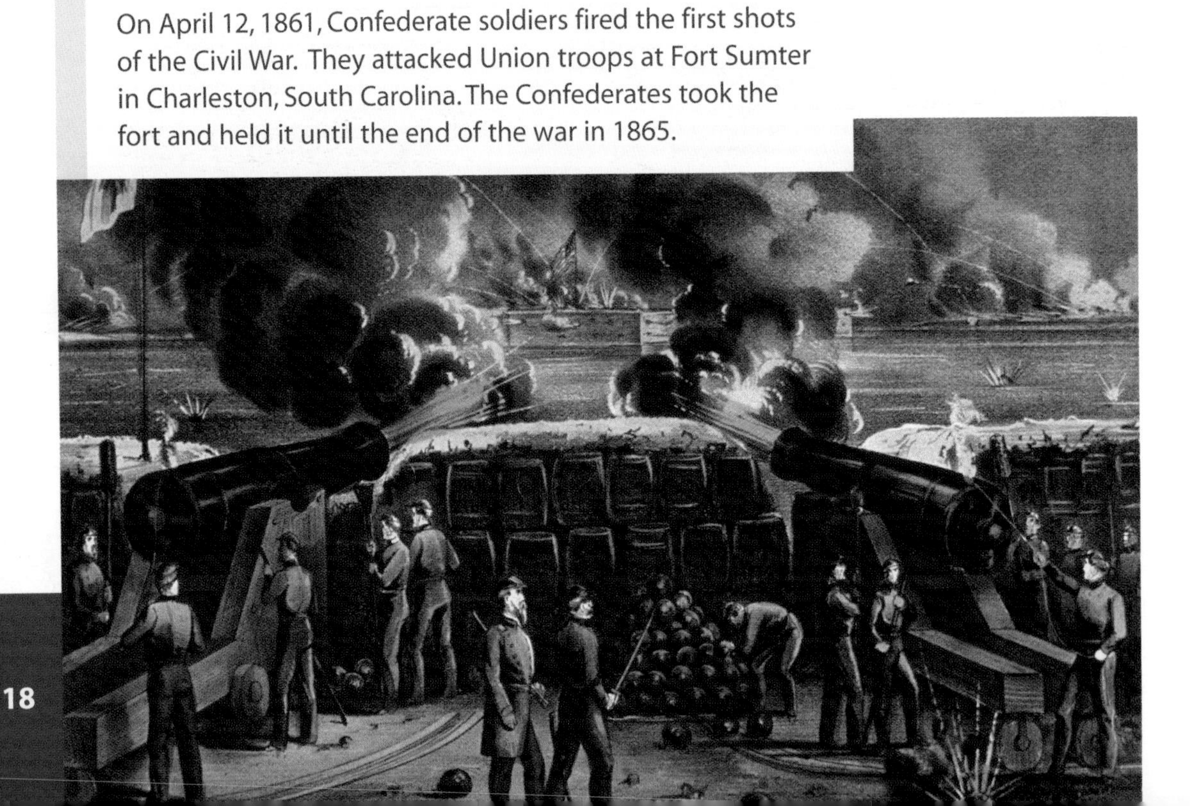

Harriet ran this hospital for escaped slaves in Beaufort, South Carolina.

These former slaves escaped when Northern troops battled their way through the South. As many as 200,000 runaways fled to Union camps, where they worked as nurses, cooks, laborers, and scouts.

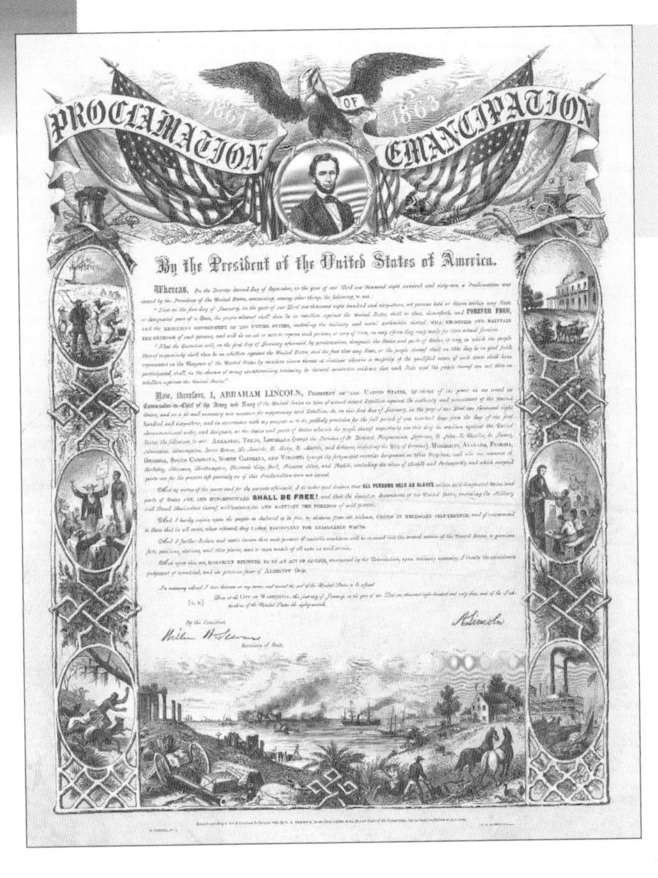

PROCLAMATION OF EMANCIPATION

1863

By the President of the United States of America.

Whereas,

FOREVER FREE,

Now, therefore, I, ABRAHAM LINCOLN,

ALL PERSONS HELD AS SLAVES

SHALL BE FREE!

This copy of the Emancipation Proclamation issued by President Abraham Lincoln is illustrated with scenes of slavery.

On January 1, 1863, there was much joy in the Union camps. President Lincoln had issued the Emancipation Proclamation. This document said all slaves in the Confederate states were now free. But everyone knew Southerners would not release their slaves that easily. There were still many battles ahead for the Union Army. By this time, many escaped slaves and free black men from the North had been trained as soldiers and organized into black **regiments**. These military units would now join the fight against the South.

Slaves set free by the Emancipation Proclamation celebrate, waving flags made from copies of the document.

Harriet became a spy for the Union Army in 1863. As a uniform, she wore a blue coat over her dress and a bandanna on her head. When she went on raids, she traded her long skirts for baggy pants called bloomers.

About this time, Union commanders called on Harriet to become a spy. As a black woman, Harriet could travel through the South unnoticed. Other blacks would trust her and most likely help her, but whites would just ignore her. Harriet picked several former slaves to be scouts for her. They searched for Confederate camps and learned the movements of enemy troops. This information helped Union commanders plan successful attacks.

About 180,000 blacks served in the Union Army. They formed 166 all-black regiments, most of which served under white commanders. Black soldiers fought in 39 battles. About 35,000 lost their lives.

In 1863, Harriet agreed to help lead a **raid** up South Carolina's Combahee River. She traveled the waterway with Colonel James Montgomery and his black regiment in three large gunboats. The group destroyed railroads and bridges to keep supplies from reaching the Confederate camps. They burned crops and buildings on plantations along the riverbanks. Hundreds of slaves fled the plantations, led by Harriet. She urged them on, singing, "Of all the whole creation in the East or in the West/The glorious Yankee nation is the greatest and the best!/Come along! Come along!" In all, the raid freed 756 slaves.

Harriet's leadership and the work of her scouts made this raid a success. Harriet knew, however, that Colonel Montgomery would receive most of the credit. She said, "Don't you think we colored people are entitled to some of the credit...We weakened the rebels somewhat on the Combahee River, by taking and bringing away [756] of their [slaves]." But Harriet never received an official "thank you" from the Union Army for her service during the Civil War, and she was paid only $200.

By the spring of 1864, Harriet was worn out. She needed a rest. She went home to Auburn, New York, where she had settled with her parents. It took several months of rest before she felt well again. She was ready to go back to the war by early 1865. But before she could reach her post in South Carolina, the war was over. The Union claimed victory and declared all slaves free.

Blacks in Washington, D.C., celebrate the end of slavery in the United States. In 1865, shortly after the Union won the Civil War, the 13th Amendment to the Constitution made slavery illegal.

Continuing the Fight

Although the Civil War had given slaves their freedom, they still struggled. Harriet continued to fight for black rights and did all she could for the newly freed slaves. She took odd jobs to earn money, but she never kept it for herself. Any amount of money she had went to help others. When former slaves showed up on her doorstep, she offered them food and shelter. She also gave money to schools for freed slaves in the South.

In 1869, when she was 47 years old, Harriet decided to marry again. Her first husband, John Tubman, had refused to follow her north. He had died in 1867. Harriet's new husband was a former Union Army soldier named Nelson Davis. He was a tall, handsome man. Although he looked healthy, he suffered from a serious lung disease called **tuberculosis**. Because of his illness, Nelson wasn't able to work. Harriet nursed him during their entire 19 years of marriage, until his death in 1888.

Harriet (far left) posed for this photograph with friends and family members in about 1888.

The Harriet Tubman Home for the Aged opened in 1908. Today, it stands as a memorial to Harriet's life and work.

In 1896, Harriet started caring for poor and elderly blacks in her own home. But she wanted to build a new house, specially made for this purpose. A plot of land came up for auction near her home in Auburn. Harriet decided to bid on the land. She later described the scene at the auction. "There were all white folks there but me," she said, "and I was there like a blackberry in a pail of milk, but I hid down in a corner, and no one knew who was bidding. . . . And then the others stopped bidding and the man said, 'All done. Who is the buyer?' 'Harriet Tubman,' I shouted."

> *"Long ago, when the Lord told me to go free my people, do you suppose he wanted me to do this just for a day, or a week? No! [He] meant me to do it just so long as I live."*
>
> —Harriet Tubman

In 1903, Harriet gave ownership of the land to her church, the African Methodist Episcopal Zion Church. The church would help build the new house. In 1908, the Harriet Tubman Home for the Aged officially opened. At first, 86-year-old Harriet worked at the home, where 12 to 15 people lived at a time. But within a few years, she became a resident there herself.

Harriet strongly believed that women should have the right to vote, and she worked for this cause into her later years. Shortly before her death, she said to a visitor, "Tell the women to stick together. God is fighting for them and all will be well!"

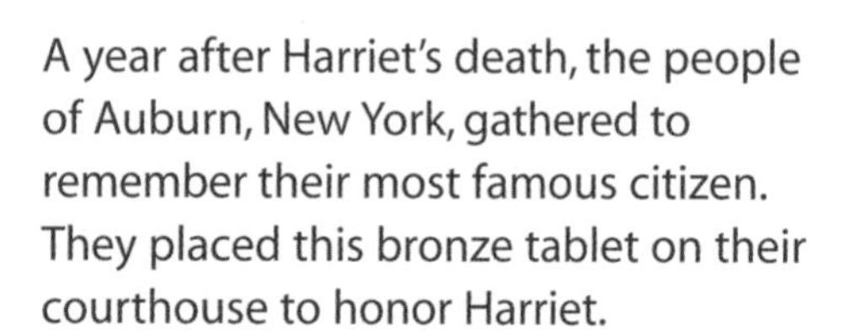

A year after Harriet's death, the people of Auburn, New York, gathered to remember their most famous citizen. They placed this bronze tablet on their courthouse to honor Harriet.

In early 1913, when Harriet was 91 years old, she felt death was near. She told people, "I can hear them bells a-ringing, I can hear the angels singing." Soon Harriet lay dying of **pneumonia**. She gathered her friends and family to her bedside to say good-bye. Harriet led them in singing "Swing Low, Sweet Chariot"—her favorite song. She died just a few days later on March 10, 1913.

Today, Harriet is remembered for living a courageous life. She never turned away from her beliefs, and she overcame every challenge she faced. Harriet Tubman was one of the greatest fighters for freedom in American history.

Did You Know?

- As many as 100,000 slaves may have escaped on the Underground Railroad between the late 1700s and Civil War times. Those who helped these "freedom seekers" were people of all backgrounds, including whites, slaves, and free blacks. They broke the law, and some even risked their own lives to help slaves travel to the North.
- Harriet was active in the women's rights movement. She met Sojourner Truth, Elizabeth Cady Stanton, and Susan B. Anthony. They fought for women's rights, particularly the right to vote. When asked if women should have the right to vote, Harriet answered that she "had suffered enough for it."
- Harriet never learned to read or write. She asked trusted friends to write letters for her.
- In 1868, a friend named Sarah Hopkins Bradford published stories about Harriet in a book titled *Scenes in the Life of Harriet Tubman*. Bradford received $1,200 for the book and gave the money to Harriet. Later, Bradford published the book again, with more information added. This book, *Harriet Tubman, the Moses of Her People*, was published in 1886.
- After her death, Harriet was buried with military honors.
- In 1944, Harriet's great niece, Evelyn Stewart Northrup, **christened** a navy ship in Harriet's honor. It was called Liberty Ship *S.S. Harriet Tubman*.
- The U.S. Postal Service issued two stamps featuring Harriet Tubman—one in 1978 and the other in 1995.

In 1995, the U.S. Postal Service issued this stamp of Harriet Tubman leading slaves to freedom. Harriet is remembered as one of America's greatest heroes.

Important Dates

Early 1822: Harriet is born on a plantation in Dorchester County, Maryland.

About 1835: An overseer strikes Harriet on the head with a lead weight. Harriet nearly dies. (age 13)

1844: Harriet marries John Tubman.

1849: Harriet escapes from slavery. (age 27)

1850: Harriet makes her first return trip to rescue her niece's family from slavery.

1851: The Fugitive Slave Act is passed.

1854: Harriet helps her three brothers escape slavery.

1857: Harriet helps her parents escape.

1861: The Civil War begins on April 12; Harriet serves as a nurse and a scout during the war. (age 39)

1863: Harriet helps lead a raid up the Combahee River in South Carolina; during the raid, 756 slaves are freed.

1864: Harriet goes home to Auburn, New York, to rest.

1865: The Civil War ends on April 9.

1868: *Scenes in the Life of Harriet Tubman* is published.

1869: Harriet marries Nelson Davis. (age 47)

1886: *Harriet Tubman, the Moses of Her People* is published.

1888: Nelson Davis dies of tuberculosis.

1908: The Harriet Tubman Home for the Aged officially opens. (age 86)

1913: Harriet dies of pneumonia. (age 91)